Simple Smoothie Recipes with Pictures

7 categories of healthy smoothies made with 5 ingredients under 300 calories

J.W.Warren

Join the Facebook Group

Simple Healthy Recipes

PRIVACY.FLOWCODE.COM

SCAN ME

- Get Free Healthy Recipes
- Stay Connected
- Get Free Recipe Books

TABLE OF CONTENTS

Introduction

WHY?

The average American's diet is honestly just pathetic. We live in the age of processed foods and unnatural additives. These heavily processed foods make up 70% of the American diet. More than 1 in 3 people in the United States are considered obese. This just blows my mind. Did you know that over 25% of kids don't drink ANY water daily? (HOW). Now, if you bought this book, I'd assume you're more healthy than the average American (so congrats). Still, as you can see, America needs to change its eating habits.

In my opinion, drinking smoothies is the best way to consume healthy foods you wouldn't normally eat. For me, it was vegetables. I would never eat them because they tasted terrible. Then my nanny started making me smoothies every day.

They were great, and little did I know they all had vegetables in them. Once she left, my smoothie-making journey began.

When I started, I just threw a bunch of ingredients in the blender and expected it to be great (ask my family, it wasn't). For the first 6 months, my smoothies were terrible; I just drank them for the nutrition. However, as time went on, I got better and better. You kind of have to get better when you use your blender over 6,000 times, no seriously, look at the picture below.

Basically, after making over 6,000 smoothies I would consider myself an "expert". Long story short, this book has been years in the making.

Nutrition

Every smoothie recipe in this book is a healthy smoothie that has specific benefits. There are 7 different categories of smoothies in this book:

1. Green Galore
2. Amazing Antioxidants
3. Detox Drinks
4. Protein Power
5. Killer Keto
6. Krazy Kids
7. Calorie Counters

Each smoothie is below 300 calories and will have the nutrition facts labeled. Understanding the nutrition facts of each smoothie will help you find your ideal smoothie. If you don't care about understanding the nutrition of the smoothies you can skip to page 36.

Calories

A calorie is a unit for measuring energy. We use calories to determine the amount of energy in food. When you hear something has 100 calories, it describes how much energy your body gets from that food.

Calories are very important because it is the secret to weight. No matter how much you think it is impossible to lose weight, it's not. Gaining and losing weight is literally a science. The most important part of calories is understanding your maintenance calories. **Your maintenance calories are the number of calories you need to eat to maintain your weight**. The average person's maintenance calories are between 1500-2500 calories.

To lose weight, you need to eat under your maintenance calories.

To maintain weight, you need to eat your maintenance calories.

To gain weight, you need to eat more than your maintenance calories.

So if your maintenance calories = 2,000

Eat < 2,000 calories to lose weight.

Eat 2,000 calories to maintain weight.

Eat > 2,000 calories to gain weight.

Scan the QR code below to to find you maintenance calories

There are many different types of calories, and not all are created equal. There are 3 main types of calories, carbohydrates, fats, and protein.

Macro Nutrients

Carbohydrates

Carbohydrates are molecules that have carbon, hydrogen, and oxygen atoms. They consist of sugar, starches, and fiber. The main purpose of carbohydrates is to provide energy for our body. Carbs come in a wide array of foods like bread, pasta, potatoes, chips, soda, oats, fruits, vegetables, and much more. **Each gram of carbohydrates contains 4 calories.**

There are two types of carbohydrates

Simple carbs

Simple Carbs (also known as refined carbs) mainly include processed sugar and refined grains. They have been stripped of their nutrients, which is why they are considered empty calories. Simple carbs lead to spikes in blood sugar and insulin levels.

Simple carbs include:

- White bread
- White rice
- Sugar
- Candy
- Cookies
- Chips
- Soda

Complex Carbs

Complex Carbs are packed with nutrients and digest much slower than simple carbs. Unlike simple carbs, complex carbs are only made of starches and fiber. Complex carbs include:

- Fruits
- Vegetables
- Whole grains
- Oats
- Rice

This book will include complex carbs such as:

- Vegetables
- Fruits
- Oats

Fats

Fats give you energy while helping your body absorb vitamins and minerals. **Every gram of fat contains 9 calories.** Many people believe diets with little to no fat are good; however, this could not be further from the truth. While some types of fat are bad for you, 20-35% of your daily calorie intake should consist of healthy fats (unless you're on the keto diet or something like that).

There are 3 types of fats:

Unsaturated Fat

This type of fat is liquid at room temperature. Unsaturated fat can improve blood cholesterol levels, ease inflammation, stabilize heart rhythms, and much more.

Unsaturated fat is primarily found in vegetable oil, nuts, and seeds. There are two types of unsaturated fat, and they are both really healthy.

Monounsaturated fat

This fat has one double bond.

Examples:

- Avocado
- Olive and peanut oil
- Almonds
- Hazelnuts
- Pecans
- Pumpkin and sesame seeds

Polyunsaturated fat

This fat has 2-6 double bonds.

Examples:

- Sunflower and flaxseed oils
- Walnuts
- Flax and chia seeds
- Fish

You can't really go wrong with unsaturated fats. I recommend that 20-30% of your calories come from unsaturated fats (for most diets).

Saturated Fats

This fat is solid at room temperature. Saturated fats are in between the great unsaturated fats and the evil trans fats. There are many debates on whether saturated fats cause heart disease and high cholesterol. However, as long as you do not consume too much of them, you will be fine. Saturated fats are found in animal products like milk, cheese, meat, and tropical oils, including coconut and palm oil.

Examples:

- Bacon
- Red meat
- Cheese
- Butter
- Regular milk
- Coconut oil

Your saturated fat intake should stay under 10% of your daily calories.

Trans Fats

Trans fat is made by heating liquid vegetable oils in the presence of hydrogen gas and a catalyst. This process is called hydrogenation which increases the fat's shelf life. Trans fat is really bad for you, and you want to consume as little as possible.

Examples:

- French fries
- Donuts
- Cookies
- Coffee creamer
- Pizza
- Microwave popcorn

This book mainly uses unsaturated fats such as:

- Avocados
- Flax Seeds
- Chia Seeds
- Peanut butter
- Almond butter

This book also uses saturated fats such as:

- Coconut oil
- Regular milk
- Heavy cream

Protein

Protein is a macronutrient made up of chemical building blocks called amino acids. Amino acids build up your bones, repair your muscles, and help create your enzymes and hormones. Your body needs protein to grow and repair cells. **Each gram of protein contains 4 calories.**

It is important that your body gets enough protein every day. The recommended daily average protein intake is:

.6—.8 grams per pound for women

.8—1.2 grams per pound for men

So a 100-pound woman should eat 60-80 grams of protein per day.

And a 200-pound man should eat 160-240 grams of protein per day.

Examples of protein include:

- Chicken
- Steak
- Fish
- Greek yogurt
- Eggs

Protein sources in this book include:

- Protein powder
- Greek yogurt
- Milk
- Peanut and almond butter

Fiber

Fiber is a carbohydrate that your body can not digest. Most carbohydrates are able to be broken down into molecules; however, fiber passes through the body undigested. Fiber helps regulate the body's use of sugars and keeps your blood sugar under control.

There are two types of Fiber:

Soluble Fiber

Soluble fiber is soluble in water and helps lower glucose levels by slowing down digestion. It also regulates the digestion of fats, which lowers bad cholesterol levels in the blood.

Soluble fiber is found in:

- Oats
- Beans
- Apples
- Blueberries
- Nuts

Insoluble Fiber

This type of fiber does not dissolve in water. Insoluble fiber helps food move through your digestive system, which helps prevent constipation.

Insoluble fiber is found in:

- Whole grains
- Brown rice
- Carrots
- Cucumbers
- Tomatoes

Most Americans get less than 15 grams of fiber per day, however, the average person should try to get 20-30 grams of fiber per day.

Sugar

Sugar is a simple carbohydrate which, as you know, has a sweet taste. When you hear the term sugar, you probably think of the white table sugar. In reality, there are a number of different sugars. There are 4 main types of sugar:

- Glucose (pasta and whole-grain sugar)
- Fructose (fruit sugar)
- Sucrose (table sugar)
- Lactose (dairy sugar)

When it comes to sugar, moderation is key. The main difference between artificial sugar and natural sugar is that fiber, nutrients, and minerals come with natural sugar. In contrast, artificial sugars are basically just empty calories. Having too much artificial sugar can lead to cardiovascular disease, higher blood sugar, weight gain, and much more.

This book mainly includes natural fructose and lactose sugars such as:

- Bananas
- Strawberries
- Pineapple
- Milk
- Yogurt

It also includes some artificial sugars such as:

- Honey
- Agave
- White sugar
- Pineapple juice

As long as your sugar comes from complex carbs packed with nutrients, then you shouldn't worry too much about your natural sugar consumption. On the flip side, try to limit your artificial sugar intake to under 30 grams per day.

Sodium

Sodium is a very important mineral found in foods. Your body needs sodium for muscle and nerve functions. It also helps keep your body fluid in balance. Even though you need sodium, most Americans get more than enough sodium every day. This is a result of processed and packaged foods having an excess amount of sodium.

Consuming too much sodium causes your body to retain more water. When you retain too much water, your organs have to work harder, leaving you at a higher risk for high blood pressure. Not to mention your face gets puffier, and you look more bloated.

Foods that are high in sodium include:

- Pizza
- Burgers
- Bacon
- Chips
- Condiments
- Most fast food

The best way to lower sodium intake is to eat low sodium foods like fruits, vegetables, whole grains, and unprocessed meats.

The average person should consume 2,000- 2,500 milligrams of sodium every day.

Blender Tips

Has your blender ever struggled to blend up your smoothie? This used to happen to me ALL the time. I just thought that I needed a stronger blender, but in reality, I just put the ingredients in the wrong order.

Ingredient Order

1. Liquids

No matter what liquid you are using (milk, water, juice, and ect), it should always be the first ingredient added. Adding in the liquid first allows the blender to create a (vortex) that pulls down the other ingredients.

2. Powders and Sweeteners

Next up are powders such as protein powder, matcha green tea, and cocoa powder or sweeteners such as honey, agave, and sugar. Adding them in second allows them to dissolve better.

3. Greens

Try and put all of your greens in third (After you wash them, obviously).
Tip: You can blend everything for 30 seconds now. This will really help out your blender, especially if it is low-medium power.

4. Soft Ingredients

Following the greens should be any soft ingredients such as fresh fruits, nut butter, and avocados.

5. Frozen Ingredients

Anything that is frozen should get added in last. This is very important and makes it easier for the blender to break up all your frozen goods.

Smoothie Hacks

Did your smoothie turn out less than ideal? You can save many of your smoothies with a little troubleshooting.

My smoothie is too thick

This is a simple fix; just add a little more liquid to the smoothie. Preferably the same liquid you already used.

My smoothie is too thin

If your smoothie comes out too thin, try using a thickener like:

- Chia Seeds
- Avocado
- Banana
- Greek yogurt
- Frozen fruit
- Nut butter

My Blender is not working

Try blending the liquids, powders, and greens before adding in the other ingredients. This will surely make the blending easier, especially if you have a low-powered blender.

My smoothie is not cold

Just throw in a few ice cubes, or try using frozen fruit and vegetables.

My smoothie is bitter

Try adding a little sweetener like honey or agave, but not too much.

My smoothie is too sweet

Add a bit of lemon or lime juice or a teaspoon of apple cider vinegar. A dash of acid will counteract the excess sweetness.

Freezing Fruit

When it comes to getting fruit for smoothies, I always prefer frozen. Benefits of frozen fruit:

- Last longer
- Retains more nutrients
- Out of season access
- You can buy in bulk
- Thickens the smoothie

Even though I prefer to use frozen fruits, it's not a big deal if you use fresh fruits. I personally use frozen fruits except for bananas (mainly because my family eats them every day). Just make sure to use ice cubes if you don't use frozen fruits. You can also freeze your greens to get the same benefits; however, I typically use fresh greens.

Preparation

When it comes to preparing your smoothies, make sure you have a:

- Blender
- Cutting board
- Sharp knife
- Measuring cups
- Container

There might be a few ingredients in this book that you do not know how to cut.
For example, I had no idea how to cut a pomegranate.

All I did was search how to cut a pomegranate on youtube, and bam (a million videos pop up). So if you are confused about how to prepare, cut or peel an ingredient, search it up on youtube. There will be a video explaining your dilemma.

Leftovers

What do you do with the leftovers?

Fresh smoothies are the best; however, sometimes, you might want to make 2-3 servings to save time. Making big servings is great, especially when multiple people are drinking them.

The main reason your smoothie will go bad is oxidation. Oxidation occurs when the smoothie is exposed to oxygen, which results in the loss of nutrients over time. Smoothies surprisingly save pretty well; just try to drink them within a day or two.

Steps to preserve the smoothie

- Pour the smoothie into a container
- Seal it (I use saran wrap; it is great)
- Preferably drink the smoothie within 24 hours

Conversions

Measurements	Ounces	Equivalents	Metric
1/4 tsp			1 ml
1/3 tsp			1.65 ml
1/2 tsp			2.5 ml
3/4 tsp			3.7 ml
1 tsp		1/3 Tbsp	5 ml
2 tsp	1/3 fl oz	2/3 Tbsp	10 ml
1/2 Tbsp	1/4 fl oz	1.5 tsp	7.5 ml
1 Tbsp	1/2 fl oz	3 tsp	15 ml
2 Tbsp	1 fl oz	6 tsp	30 ml
1/4 cup	2 fl oz	4 Tbsp	60 ml
1/3 cup	2.66 fl oz		80 ml
1/2 cup	4 fl oz	8 Tbsp	120ml
2/3 cup	5.33 fl oz		160 ml
3/4 cup	6 fl oz	12 Tbsp	180ml
1 cup	8 fl oz	16 Tbsp	240 ml

REVIEW

★★★★★

If you have been enjoying the book, a review would be very apreciated

SCAN ME

Green Galore

Welcome to the first section of the book; Green Galore. The Green Galore smoothies are green smoothies containing healthy green vegetables. Many of the smoothies hide the taste of the greens, while a few embrace the green taste.

Greens have many benefits such as:

- Contains lots of vitamins and nutrients
- Reduces inflammation
- Makes your skin glow
- Boost the immune system
- Helps digestive enzymes
- Supports bone health
- Low calorie
- and much more

As you can see, greens are very healthy. My favorite way (hands down) to consume greens is through green smoothies.

GREEN GALORE

Broccoli Grape

20 oz or 600 ml

INGREDIENTS:

- ¾ cup or 175 ml of almond milk
- 1 cup or 75g of broccoli
- 1 banana
- 1 cup or 145g of green grapes
- 3-5 ice cubes

NUTRITIONAL INFORMATION

- Calories 237
- Fat 2g
- Saturated fat 0g
- Carbohydrates 49g
- Fiber 5g
- Sugar 33g
- Protein 3g

GREEN GALORE

Tropical Broccoli

14 oz or 415 ml

INGREDIENTS:

- ¼ cup or 60 ml of pineapple juice
- ¾ cup or 175ml of water
- ¾ cup or 55g of broccoli
- ½ of a banana
- ½ cup or 70g of frozen mango
- ¼ cup or 35g of frozen strawberries

NUTRITIONAL INFORMATION

- Calories 155
- Fat 0g
- Saturated fat 0g
- Carbohydrates 35g
- Fiber 5g
- Sugar 24g
- Protein 2g

GREEN GALORE

Avocado Spinach

15 oz or 450 ml

INGREDIENTS:

- ¾ cup or 175 ml of almond milk
- 2 cups or 56g of spinach
- ¼ of an avocado
- 1 banana
- ½ of an apple
- 3-5 ice cubes

NUTRITIONAL INFORMATION

- Calories 265
- Fat 8g
- Saturated fat 1g
- Carbohydrates 47g
- Fiber 9g
- Sugar 27g
- Protein 5g

GREEN GALORE

Spicy Mango

10 oz or 300 ml

INGREDIENTS:

- 1 cup or 240 ml of almond milk
- 1 cup or 28g of spinach
- 1 teaspoon or 2g of ginger
- 1 cup or 120g of frozen mango
- a small pinch of cayenne pepper (depends on your tolerance)

NUTRITIONAL INFORMATION

- Calories 149
- Fat 3g
- Saturated fat 0g
- Carbohydrates 30g
- Fiber 3g
- Sugar 26g
- Protein 3g

GREEN GALORE

Celery Pear

17.5 oz or 520 ml

INGREDIENTS:

- 1 cup or 240 ml of water
- 1 cup or 28g of spinach
- ⅓ cup or 30g of chopped celery
- 1 medium pear
- 5 ice cubes

NUTRITIONAL INFORMATION

- Calories 114
- Fat 0g
- Saturated fat 0g
- Carbohydrates 29g
- Fiber 7g
- Sugar 18g
- Protein 2g

GREEN GALORE

Cucumber Kale

8.5 oz or 250 ml

INGREDIENTS:

- ½ cup or 120 ml of water
- 1 cup or 30g of kale
- 1 cup or 120g of sliced cucumber
- 2 tablespoons or 20g of flax seeds
- 5 ice cubes

NUTRITIONAL INFORMATION

- Calories 159
- Fat 9g
- Saturated fat 0g
- Carbohydrates 15g
- Fiber 8g
- Sugar 4g
- Protein 7g

GREEN
GALORE

Kale Cantaloupe

17 oz or 500 ml

INGREDIENTS:

- ¼ cup or 60 ml of almond milk
- 1 ½ cup of kale
- 1 banana
- 1 cup or 45g of cantaloupe
- 3-4 ice cubes

NUTRITIONAL INFORMATION

- Calories 219
- Fat 2g
- Saturated fat 0g
- Carbohydrates 47g
- Fiber 8g
- Sugar 29g
- Protein 7g

GREEN GALORE

Pineapple Kale

23.5 oz or 700 ml

INGREDIENTS:

- 1 cup or 240 ml of almond milk (unsweetened)
- ½ cup or 120 ml of pineapple juice
- 1 cup or 30g of kale
- 1 banana
- ½ cup or 70g of frozen pineapple
- 1-2 ice cubes

NUTRITIONAL INFORMATION

- Calories 264
- Fat 4g
- Saturated fat 0g
- Carbohydrates 55g
- Fiber 7g
- Sugar 33g
- Protein 5g

GREEN
GALORE

Orange Kale

19 oz or 560 ml

INGREDIENTS:

- ¾ cup or 175 ml
  of water
- ½ cup or 120 ml
  of orange juice
- ½ cup or 15 ml
  of kale
- ¼ of an avocado
- ½ a banana
- 1 cup or 120g
  of frozen mango chunks

NUTRITIONAL INFORMATION

- Calories 260
- Fat 6g
- Saturated fat 1g
- Carbohydrates 51g
- Fiber 8g
- Sugar 38g
- Protein 5g

GREEN GALORE

Mango Arugula

20.5 oz or 610 ml

INGREDIENTS:

- ¾ cup or 175 ml of coconut water
- 1 cup or 28g of arugula
- 1 teaspoon or 2g of coconut shreds
- ½ of an avocado
- 1 cup or 120g of frozen mango
- 1-2 ice cubes

* ½ of a lime (zest and juice) **optional***

NUTRITIONAL INFORMATION

- Calories 284
- Fat 15g
- Saturated fat 5g
- Carbohydrates 40g
- Fiber 5g
- Sugar 28g
- Protein 4g

Amazing Antioxidants

This section has smoothies loaded with antioxidants. Antioxidants are chemical compounds that protect your cells from damage by free radicals (which are unstable molecules). Free Radicals are very dangerous and can cause:

- Cardiovascular disease
- Inflammatory disease
- Cataracts
- Cancer

Due to free radicals lacking electrons, they steal electrons from other molecules and damage those molecules in the process. Antioxidants neutralize free radicals by giving up some of their own electrons. This helps break a chain reaction that can be very damaging to the molecules in the body.

Amazing Antioxidants

Antioxidants can be found in

- Green vegetables
- Blueberries
- Cherries
- Oranges
- Pomegranate
- Watermelon
- Grapefruit
- Raspberries
- Blackberries
- Matcha green tea powder
- and much more

Most of the ingredients in these smoothies contain a high amount of antioxidants.

AMAZING ANTIOXIDANTS

Blueberry Kale

10 oz or 300 ml

INGREDIENTS:

- ½ cup or 120ml of water
- ½ cup or 15g of kale
- 1 tablespoon or 10g of flax seeds
- ½ a banana
- ½ cup or 75g of frozen blueberries
- 1-2 ice cubes

NUTRITIONAL INFORMATION

- Calories 159
- Fat 5g
- Saturated fat 0g
- Carbohydrates 28g
- Fiber 8g
- Sugar 14g
- Protein 4g

AMAZING ANTIOXIDANTS

Blueberry Vanilla

17 oz or 500 ml

INGREDIENTS:

- ¾ cup or 175 ml of almond milk
- 1 teaspoon or 5 ml of vanilla extract
- 1 tablespoon or 10g of flax seeds
- 1 banana
- 1 cup or 150g of frozen blueberries
- 2-4 ice cubes

NUTRITIONAL INFORMATION

- Calories 285
- Fat 8g
- Saturated fat 1g
- Carbohydrates 53g
- Fiber 10g
- Sugar 32g
- Protein 4g

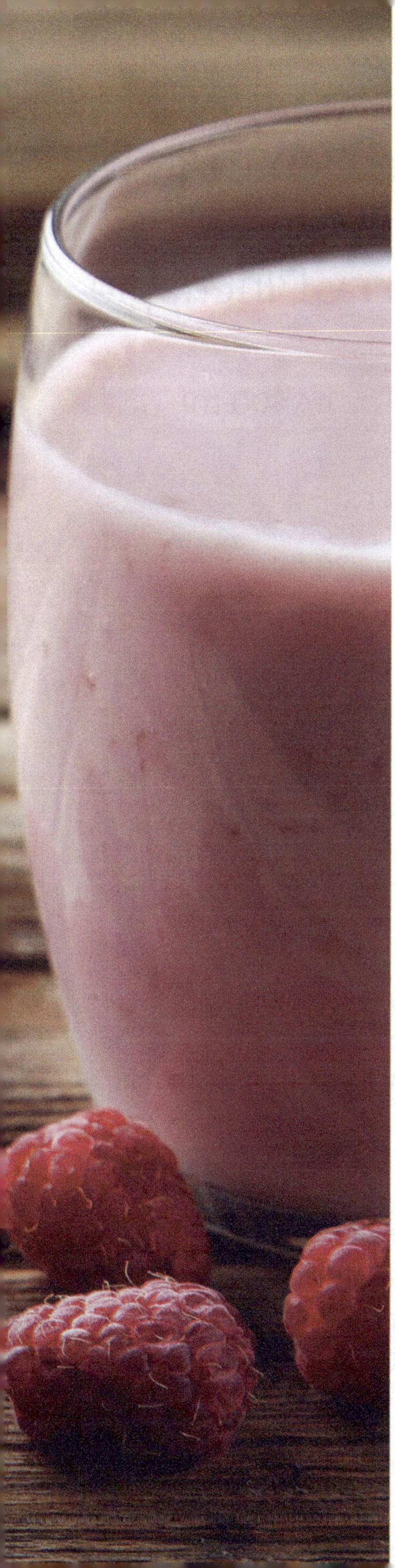

AMAZING ANTIOXIDANTS

Raspberry Peach

13.5 oz or 400 ml

INGREDIENTS:

- 1 cup or 240 ml of almond milk
- 1 teaspoon or 5 ml of honey
- ½ cup or 70g of raspberries
- 1 cup or 130g of frozen peaches
- 3-4 ice cubes

NUTRITIONAL INFORMATION

- Calories 173
- Fat 3g
- Saturated fat 0g
- Carbohydrates 34g
- Fiber 6g
- Sugar 24g
- Protein 2g

AMAZING ANTIOXIDANTS

Blackberry Pineapple

13.5 oz or 400 ml

INGREDIENTS:

- ½ cup or 120 ml of almond milk
- ¼ cup or 60 ml of plain non-fat Greek yogurt
- 1 tablespoon or 15 ml of honey
- ¾ cup or 110g of blackberries
- ½ cup or 70g of frozen pineapples

NUTRITIONAL INFORMATION

- Calories 275
- Fat 2g
- Saturated fat 0g
- Carbohydrates 53g
- Fiber 8g
- Sugar 40g
- Protein 15g

AMAZING ANTIOXIDANTS

Ginger Grapefruit

20 oz or 600 ml

INGREDIENTS:

- ½ cup or 120 ml of pineapple juice
- 1 cup or 200g of grapefruit
- ½ teaspoon or 1g of ginger
- 1 cup or 140g of frozen pineapple

NUTRITIONAL INFORMATION

- Calories 210
- Fat 2g
- Saturated fat 0g
- Carbohydrates 53g
- Fiber 5g
- Sugar 43g
- Protein 2g

AMAZING ANTIOXIDANTS

Ginger Cucumber

12 oz or 350 ml

INGREDIENTS:

- ¾ cup or 140 ml of coconut water
- 1 cup or 120g of sliced cucumber
- 1 tablespoon or 15 ml of honey
- 1 cup or 135g of strawberries
- 1 teaspoon or 2g of ginger

NUTRITIONAL INFORMATION

- Calories 197
- Fat 1g
- Saturated fat 0g
- Carbohydrates 48g
- Fiber 8g
- Sugar 40g
- Protein 1g

AMAZING ANTIOXIDANTS

Watermelon Rosemary

17 oz or 500 ml

INGREDIENTS:

- 1 cup or 140g of seedless watermelon
- 1 medium orange
- ¾ teaspoon or 1g of rosemary
- 1 cup or 135g of frozen strawberries

NUTRITIONAL INFORMATION

- Calories 159
- Fat 0g
- Saturated fat 0g
- Carbohydrates 40g
- Fiber 7g
- Sugar 31g
- Protein 2g

AMAZING ANTIOXIDANTS

Pomegranate Pineapple

11 oz or 325 ml

INGREDIENTS:

- 2.5 tablespoons or 35 ml of plain greek yogurt
- ¾ of a teaspoon or 4 ml of maple syrup
- ½ cup or 70g of pomegranate seeds
- ½ of a banana
- ½ cup or 70g of frozen pineapple
- 2-3 ice cubes

NUTRITIONAL INFORMATION

- Calories 196
- Fat 1g
- Saturated fat 0g
- Carbohydrates 45g
- Fiber 4g
- Sugar 35g
- Protein 5g

AMAZING ANTIOXIDANTS

Chocolate Cherry

17 oz or 500 ml

INGREDIENTS:

- 1 cup or 240 ml of almond milk
- 1 tablespoon or 7g of cocoa powder
- 1 teaspoon or 18g of almond butter
- 1 date
- 1 cup or 135 g of **frozen** black cherries (**Frozen cherries come pitted.**)
- 4-5 ice cubes

NUTRITIONAL INFORMATION

- Calories 288
- Fat 12g
- Saturated fat 1g
- Carbohydrates 45g
- Fiber 5g
- Sugar 35g
- Protein 6g

AMAZING ANTIOXIDANTS

Green Tea

20 oz or 600 ml

INGREDIENTS:

- ¾ cup or 175 ml of coconut milk
- 2 teaspoons or 4g of Matcha green tea powder
- 1 tablespoon or 15 ml of maple syrup
- 1 banana
- 1 cup or 130g of frozen peaches
- 1-3 ice cubes

NUTRITIONAL INFORMATION

- Calories 289
- Fat 4g
- Saturated fat 3g
- Carbohydrates 61g
- Fiber 9g
- Sugar 36g
- Protein 6g

Detox Drinks

All of the smoothies in this chapter are designed to remove toxins from your body. Detox smoothies will help cleanse your body, which allows you to feel better and more energized. Toxins get into your body through the air you breathe and unhealthy foods high in fat, sugar, sodium, and additives. This chapter includes many acidic fruits such as:

- Grapefruit
- Pineapple
- Lemon
- Oranges
- Peaches

Acids in these fruits will help flush out toxins, improve your metabolic functions, prevent ailments, and more. It is important to know that detoxification will not occur unless you pair these smoothies with a healthy and balanced diet. Toxins harm your body, and it is really important to get rid of them.

DETOX DRINKS

Minty Beet

7.5 oz or 225 ml

INGREDIENTS:

- 2/3 cup or 155 ml of apple juice
- ⅓ of a beet
- ¼ of a banana
- 1 ⅓ cup or 175 ml of frozen strawberries
- 1 teaspoon or .66g of mint

NUTRITIONAL INFORMATION

- Calories 185
- Fat 0g
- Saturated fat 0g
- Carbohydrates 46g
- Fiber 6g
- Sugar 37g
- Protein 2g

Beet Berries

20 oz or 600 ml

INGREDIENTS:

- 1 cup or 240 ml of coconut milk
- ½ of a banana
- 1 cup or 130g of raw beet
- ½ cup or 75g of frozen blue berries
- ½ a cup or 70g of frozen strawberries

NUTRITIONAL INFORMATION

- Calories 213
- Fat 5g
- Saturated fat 4g
- Carbohydrates 41g
- Fiber 10g
- Sugar 26g
- Protein 3g

DETOX DRINKS

Tropical Lime

19 oz 570 ml

INGREDIENTS:

- 1 ¼ cup or 300 ml of coconut water
- ¼ cup or 60 ml of lime juice
- 1 cup or 28g of spinach
- 1 cup or 140g of frozen pineapple
- 1 cup or 140g of frozen mango

NUTRITIONAL INFORMATION

- Calories 232
- Fat 1g
- Saturated fat 1g
- Carbohydrates 60g
- Fiber 8g
- Sugar 48g
- Protein 3g

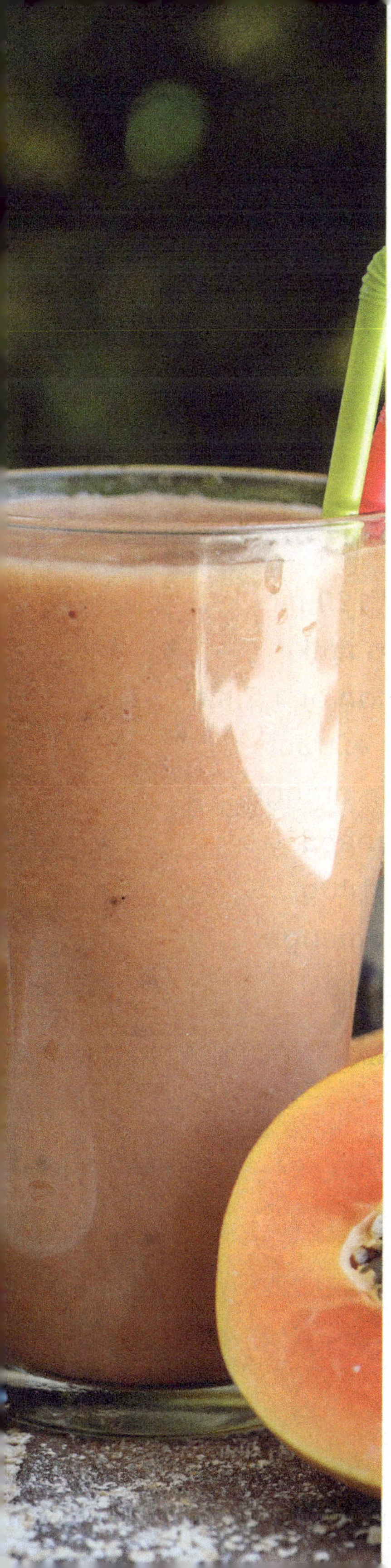

DETOX DRINKS

Papaya Mango

21 oz or 620 ml

INGREDIENTS:

- ½ cup or 120 ml of coconut milk
- ½ cup or 120 ml of water
- 1 banana
- 1 cup or 140g of chopped papaya
- 1 cup or 140g of frozen mango
- 3-4 ice cubes

NUTRITIONAL INFORMATION

- Calories 275
- Fat 5g
- Saturated fat 4g
- Carbohydrates 59g
- Fiber 7g
- Sugar 40g
- Protein 4g

Vanilla Orange

20 oz or 620 ml

INGREDIENTS:

- ½ cup or 120 ml of almond milk
- ¼ teaspoon or 1.2 ml of vanilla extract
- 1 medium orange
- ½ of a banana
- 1 cup or 140g of frozen mango
- 3-4 ice cubes

NUTRITIONAL INFORMATION

-

Cinnamon Peach

8 oz or 240 ml

INGREDIENTS:

- ¾ cup or 175 ml of coconut milk
- ½ cup or 120 ml of vanilla greek yogurt
- ¼ teaspoon or .75g of cinnamon
- 1 cup or 130g of frozen peaches

NUTRITIONAL INFORMATION

- Calories 182
- Fat 4g
- Saturated fat 3g
- Carbohydrates 27g
- Fiber 4g
- Sugar 23g
- Protein 11g

DETOX DRINKS

Ginger Green Tea

11 oz or 340 ml

INGREDIENTS:

- ½ cup or 120 ml of unsweetened almond milk
- 2 tablespoons or 30 ml of lemon juice
- 2 teaspoons or 4g of matcha green tea powder
- 1 ½ teaspoon or 3g of ginger
- 1 apple
- 3-4 ice cubes

optional 1 tablespoon or 15 ml of honey

NUTRITIONAL INFORMATION

- Calories 153
- Fat 2g
- Saturated fat 0g
- Carbohydrates 34g
- Fiber 8g
- Sugar 19g
- Protein 5g

DETOX DRINKS

Orange Ginger Spice

10 oz or 300 ml

INGREDIENTS:

- ½ cup or 120 ml of water
- ½ teaspoon or 1g of powdered turmeric
- A pinch of black pepper
- 1 teaspoon or 2g of ginger
- ⅓ cup or 45g of chopped carrots
- 1 peeled orange
- 3-4 ice cubes

NUTRITIONAL INFORMATION

- Calories 88
- Fat 0g
- Saturated fat 0g
- Carbohydrates 21g
- Fiber 5g
- Sugar 14g
- Protein 2g

DETOX DRINKS

Chai Tea

13.5 oz or 400 ml

INGREDIENTS:

- 1 cup or 240 ml of oat milk
- ½ teaspoon or .75g of chai tea powder
- 2 teaspoons or 20g of chia seeds
- 1 banana
- 3-4 ice cubes

NUTRITIONAL INFORMATION

- Calories 234
- Fat 7g
- Saturated fat 0g
- Carbohydrates 40g
- Fiber 5g
- Sugar 26g
- Protein 3g

DETOX DRINKS

Zucchini Cucumber

19.5 oz or 580 ml

INGREDIENTS:

- 1 cup or 240 ml of water
- ½ cup or 60g of chopped cucumber
- ½ cup or 60g of chopped zucchini
- ¼ of an avocado
- 1 kiwi
- 3-4 ice cubes

NUTRITIONAL INFORMATION

- Calories 123
- Fat 6g
- Saturated fat 1g
- Carbohydrates 16g
- Fiber 5g
- Sugar 8g
- Protein 3g

Protein Power

This section of the book consists of smoothies with protein powder. So basically, these are just good tasting protein shakes. It is really important to get enough protein every day.
Protein:

- Aids in injury recovery
- Reduces muscle loss
- Builds lean muscle
- Curbs hunger

Drinking protein is the easiest way to add more protein to your diet. If you don't eat enough protein, try implementing a protein smoothie into your diet.

PROTEIN POWER

Vanilla Kicker

10 oz or 300 ml

INGREDIENTS:

- 2/3 cup or 155 ml of milk
- 1 cup or 28g of spinach
- 1 teaspoon or 4g of chia seeds
- 2 tablespoons or 15g of vanilla protein powder
- 1 cup or 140g of any tropical frozen fruit mix

NUTRITIONAL INFORMATION

- Calories 293
- Fat 8g
- Saturated fat 3g
- Carbohydrates 36g
- Fiber 8g
- Sugar 23g
- Protein 21g

PROTEIN POWER

Strawberry Protein

10.5 oz or 315 ml

INGREDIENTS:

- ½ cup or 120 ml of milk
- 2 tablespoons or 15g of any protein powder
- ½ tablespoon or 25g of peanut butter
- ½ of a banana
- ¼ cup or 35g of frozen strawberries
- 3-4 ice cubes

NUTRITIONAL INFORMATION

- Calories 275
- Fat 11g
- Saturated fat 4g
- Carbohydrates 24g
- Fiber 2g
- Sugar 14g
- Protein 21g

PROTEIN POWER

Purple Power

17 oz or 500 ml

INGREDIENTS:

- 1 cup or 240 ml of unsweetened almond milk
- 1 scoop of vanilla protein powder
- ½ of a banana
- ¾ cup or 110g of frozen mixed berries
- 1-2 ice cubes

NUTRITIONAL INFORMATION

- Calories 255
- Fat 4g
- Saturated fat 1g
- Carbohydrates 31g
- Fiber 5g
- Sugar 16g
- Protein 26g

PROTEIN POWER

Kiwi Spinach

18 oz or 530 ml

INGREDIENTS:

- 1 cup or 240 ml of unsweetened almond milk
- ¼ cup or 60 ml of water
- 1 cup or 28g of spinach
- 1 banana
- 1 Kiwi
- 1 scoop of vanilla protein powder
- 3-4 ice cubes

NUTRITIONAL INFORMATION

- Calories 299
- Fat 4g
- Saturated fat 1g
- Carbohydrates 39g
- Fiber 6g
- Sugar 19g
- Protein 28g

PROTEIN POWER

Grey Protein

7 oz or 200 ml

INGREDIENTS:

- ½ cup or 120 ml of coconut milk
- 1 cup or 28g of spinach
- ½ a banana
- ½ a scoop of chocolate protein powder
- 3-4 ice cubes

NUTRITIONAL INFORMATION

- Calories 142
- Fat 3g
- Saturated fat 3g
- Carbohydrates 15g
- Fiber 2g
- Sugar 9g
- Protein 14g

Killer Keto

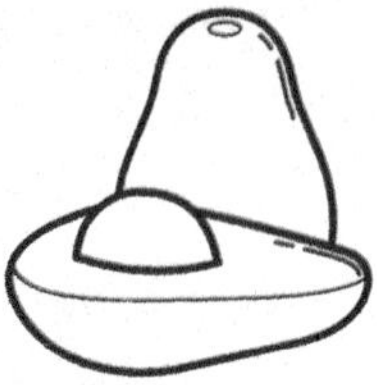

This section of the book contains smoothies that fit into the Ketogenic diet. A keto diet (also known as a "low-carb/high-fat diet") forces the body into a state of ketosis. Ketosis is where your body uses fats as the main source of fuel, which allows you to burn fat at a higher rate. So all of these smoothies are low in carbs and sugar.

Fats are very saturating, so the Keto smoothies will leave you feeling full and satisfied. These are not the sweetest smoothies; however, they are packed with minerals and nutrients. This section is great if you are on the Keto diet or looking to cut back on carbs.

KILLER KETO

Cocoa Almond Butter

7 oz or 200 ml

INGREDIENTS:

- ½ cup or 120 ml of unsweetened almond milk
- ½ tablespoon or 2.5g of raw cocoa powder
- ½ tablespoon or 8g of sugar
- ½ tablespoon or 8g of coconut oil
- 1 ½ tbsp or 27g of almond butter
- 3-5 ice cubes

NUTRITIONAL INFORMATION

- Calories 247
- Fat 22g
- Saturated fat 8g
- Carbohydrates 12g
- Fiber 3g
- Sugar 7g
- Protein 5g

KILLER KETO

Raspberry Coconut

13.5 oz or 400 ml

INGREDIENTS:

- 1 cup or 240 ml of unsweetened almond milk
- 1 cup or 28g of spinach
- 1 tablespoon or 16g of coconut oil
- 1/8 teaspoon or .4g of cinnamon
- ½ cup or 70g of raspberries
- 3-5 ice cubes

NUTRITIONAL INFORMATION

- Calories 189
- Fat 17g
- Saturated fat 12g
- Carbohydrates 9g
- Fiber 6g
- Sugar 3g
- Protein 3g

KILLER KETO

Strawberry Cream

10 oz or 300 ml

INGREDIENTS:

- ¾ cup or 175 ml of unsweetened almond milk
- ¼ cup or 60 ml of heavy cream
- ½ tablespoon or 7ml of agave
- 1 teaspoon or 15ml of vanilla extract
- 1/3 cup or 45g of frozen strawberries
- 2-3 ice cubes

NUTRITIONAL INFORMATION

- Calories 279
- Fat 26g
- Saturated fat 14g
- Carbohydrates 13g
- Fiber 2g
- Sugar 10g
- Protein 1g

KILLER KETO

Avocado

20 oz or 600 ml

INGREDIENTS:

- 1 1/2 cups or 360 ml of water
- 1 tablespoon or 15 ml of lime juice
- 1 teaspoon or 1g of lime zest
- 1 tablespoon or 15 ml of maple syrup
- 1 medium avocado
- 4-5 ice cubes

NUTRITIONAL INFORMATION

- Calories 263
- Fat 21g
- Saturated fat 3g
- Carbohydrates 20g
- Fiber 10g
- Sugar 8g
- Protein 3g

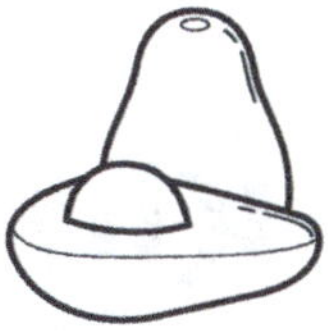

KILLER
KETO

Keto Lime

7oz or 200 ml

INGREDIENTS:

- ½ cup or 120 ml of unsweetened almond milk
- 1 cup or 28g of spinach
- 2 tablespoons or 30 ml of lime juice
- 2 tablespoons or 12g of shredded coconut
- ¼ cup or 35g of raw cashews
- 5 ice cubes

NUTRITIONAL INFORMATION

- Calories 265
- Fat 22g
- Saturated fat 10g
- Carbohydrates 15g
- Fiber 4g
- Sugar 2g
- Protein 7g

Krazy Kids

This section of the book has simple smoothies that even the plainest of palates will enjoy. We all know how hard it can be for a kid to eat food. Yet alone, it's even harder to get them to eat healthy, nutritious foods. Most parents just sacrifice and feed their kids fast and processed food because it is easy.

However, it is very easy to get a kid to drink a smoothie. Smoothies are my favorite way to feed picky eaters. You can even sneak kale and spinach in without them even questioning. If you have kids or just like simple and easy smoothies, this is a great chapter for you.

Scan the qr code to leave a review any feedback really helps out.

KRAZY KIDS

Mango Peach

23.5 oz or 700 ml

INGREDIENTS:

- 1 ½ cup or 355 ml of almond milk
- ½ teaspoon or 2 ml of vanilla extract
- 1 cup or 130g of frozen peaches
- 1 cup or 140g of frozen mangos
- 2-3 ice cubes

Optional 1 cup or 28g of spinach

NUTRITIONAL INFORMATION

- Calories 234
- Fat 4g
- Saturated fat 0g
- Carbohydrates 50g
- Fiber 5g
- Sugar 43g
- Protein 3g

KRAZY KIDS

Strawberry Kiwi

17.5 oz or 520 ml

INGREDIENTS:

- ¾ cup or 175ml of pineapple and orange juice blend
- ½ cup or 120 ml of strawberry or vanilla greek yogurt
- 1 kiwi (green or golden)
- ½ cup or 70g of strawberries
- 2-3 ice cubes

NUTRITIONAL INFORMATION

- Calories 246
- Fat 3g
- Saturated fat 1g
- Carbohydrates 46g
- Fiber 4g
- Sugar 34g
- Protein 11g

KRAZY KIDS

Pineapple Banana

23.5 oz or 700 ml

INGREDIENTS:

- ½ cup or 120 ml of water
- ½ cup or 120 ml of vanilla greek yogurt
- 1 banana
- 1 cup or 140g of frozen pineapple
- 2-3 ice cubes

NUTRITIONAL INFORMATION

- Calories 278
- Fat 2g
- Saturated fat 1g
- Carbohydrates 57g
- Fiber 6g
- Sugar 37g
- Protein 11g

KRAZY KIDS

Peanut Butter Banana

10 oz or 300 ml

INGREDIENTS:

- ½ cup or 120 ml of coconut milk
- ½ a banana
- ¼ cup or 20g of oats
- ½ tablespoon or 25g of peanut butter
- 1 date
- 3-5 ice cubes

NUTRITIONAL INFORMATION

- Calories 235
- Fat 8g
- Saturated fat 4g
- Carbohydrates 38g
- Fiber 5g
- Sugar 16g
- Protein 6g

KRAZY KIDS

Grapefruit Banana

17 oz or 500 ml

INGREDIENTS:

- ½ cup or 120 ml of orange juice
- ½ cup or 120 ml of coconut water
- 1 banana
- ½ cup or 100g of grapefruit
- 3-4 ice cubes

NUTRITIONAL INFORMATION

- Calories 214
- Fat 1g
- Saturated fat 0g
- Carbohydrates 38g
- Fiber 4g
- Sugar 29g
- Protein 2g

KRAZY KIDS

Apple Cinnamon

10 oz or 300 ml

INGREDIENTS:

- ½ a cup or 120 ml of coconut milk
- ¼ teaspoon or 1 ml of vanilla extract
- ½ teaspoon or 1.5g of cinnamon
- 1 tablespoon or 50g of peanut butter
- ½ of an apple
- 3-4 ice cubes

NUTRITIONAL INFORMATION

- Calories 182
- Fat 12g
- Saturated fat 5g
- Carbohydrates 18g
- Fiber 3g
- Sugar 11g
- Protein 4g

Calorie Counters

I realize that a lot of these smoothies are in the 200-300 calorie range, and for some (THATS ALOT). That is why I have made the calorie counter section. These smoothies are all below 100 calories and loaded with healthy nutrients.

While the smoothies are very limited, there is always room to keep things interesting while keeping the calories low. These smoothies are great for breakfast or a quick snack. They might not be the sweetest smoothies, but if you are really trying to lose weight, these are the smoothies for you.

CALORIE COUNTERS

★ Ginger Apple

13.5 oz or 400 ml

INGREDIENTS:

- ⅓ cup or 75ml of water
- 2 cups or 56g of spinach
- 1 cup or 120g of sliced cucumber
- 1 teaspoon or .66g of mint leaves
- ¼ teaspoon or .5g of ginger
- ½ of an apple
- 4-5 ice cubes

NUTRITIONAL INFORMATION

- Calories 83
- Fat 1g
- Saturated fat 0g
- Carbohydrates 19g
- Fiber 5g
- Sugar 12g
- Protein 3g

CALORIE COUNTERS

Mixed Berries

10 oz or 300 ml

INGREDIENTS:

- ½ cup or 120 ml of coconut milk
- ½ cup or 75g of frozen blueberries
- ½ cup or 70g of frozen strawberries

NUTRITIONAL INFORMATION

- Calories 99
- Fat 3g
- Saturated fat 3g
- Carbohydrates 18g
- Fiber 4g
- Sugar 13g
- Protein 1g

CALORIE COUNTERS

Tropical Tea

13.5 oz or 400 ml

INGREDIENTS:

- 1 ¼ cup or 300 ml of green tea
- ¼ cup or 30g of frozen peaches
- ¼ cup or 30g of frozen mangos
- ½ cup or 70g of frozen strawberries

NUTRITIONAL INFORMATION

- Calories 84
- Fat 1g
- Saturated fat 0g
- Carbohydrates 20g
- Fiber 4g
- Sugar 14g
- Protein 2g

CALORIE COUNTERS

Expresso Date

13.5 oz or 400 ml

INGREDIENTS:

- ½ cup or 120 ml of unsweetened almond milk
- 1-2 teaspoons or 1-2g of expresso
- ½ of a banana
- 1 date
- 3-4 ice cubes

NUTRITIONAL INFORMATION

- Calories 95
- Fat 1g
- Saturated fat 0g
- Carbohydrates 19g
- Fiber 2g
- Sugar 10g
- Protein 1g

CALORIE COUNTERS

Watermelon Strawberry

7 oz or 200 ml

INGREDIENTS:

- ¾ cup or 105g of watermelon
  *****blend the watermelon before putting in the strawberries, this will make it easier for the blender*****
- ½ cup or 70g of frozen strawberries

NUTRITIONAL INFORMATION

- Calories 59
- Fat 0g
- Saturated fat 0g
- Carbohydrates 15g
- Fiber 2g
- Sugar 11g
- Protein 1g

Key to Loosing Weight

You can drink all the healthy smoothies in the world, but if the rest of your lifestyle is not healthy, there will be no progress. So many times I see people get one aspect of their health and fitness journey down while neglecting the others. For example, I have a lot of friends who work out all the time, but take nutrition as a joke. Yeah, this might work until your early 20's, but as a lot of you know, it catches up.

Achieving your goals, especially fitness goals, requires hard work, dedication, and mostly consistency. The only way you lose is when you quit. When it comes to health and fitness, I believe that nutrition is the most important aspect and smoothies are the BEST way to get in healthy food that might not be the most appetizing (Broccoli and Kale).

Smoothies can help you

- Lose fat
- Gain muscle
- Balance out your diet
- Eat on the go
- Not do as many dishes*
- Eat bad tasting healthy foods
- Feel better

So keep making your smoothies, and as time goes on, you will improve (I promise). Implement these smoothies into your healthy diet and start seeing the progress you have always wanted.

MEET THE AUTHOR

James Warren is a young author/ entrepreneur who, at the time of this book, just finished his freshman year at Texas Tech. James has been into health and nutrition for 5 years, and it is one of his many passions. As an author, his goal is to make recipe books that educate the reader about proper nutrition; while providing healthy recipes. If you enjoyed the book, feel free to leave a review, it would really help out!

Leave a Review below

willwarren11

Sources

"Average American Diet Statistics in 2022." ABECSW.org, 2 June 2021, www.abecsw.org.

"Adult Obesity Facts." Centers for Disease Control and Prevention, Centers for Disease Control and Prevention, 30 Sept. 2021, www.cdc.gov.

"Ranking (% Obesity by Country)." World Obesity Federation Global Obesity Observatory, data.worldobesity.org.

Gunnars, Kris. "Confused about Whether You Should Eat Carbs or Not? Here's the Lowdown." Healthline, Healthline Media, 14 July 2021, www.healthline.com.

"Simple Carbs vs. Complex Carbs: What's the Difference?" Medical News Today, MediLexicon International, www.medicalnewstoday.com.

"Types of Fat." The Nutrition Source, 24 July 2018, www.hsph.harvard.edu.

"Types of Fats." Types of Fats | Michigan Medicine, www.uofmhealth.org.

"Keto Smoothies." Konscious Keto, konsciousketo.com

"Protein." Protein - Better Health Channel, www.betterhealth.vic.gov.

"Learning about Calories (for Kids) - Nemours Kidshealth." Edited by Mary L. Gavin, KidsHealth, The Nemours Foundation, June 2018, kidshealth.org.

Https://Www.verywellfit.com/Common-Questions-about-Calories-2506644#:~:Text=The%20number%20of%20calories%20you,to%202%2C500%20calories%20per%20day.&Text=If%20you%20want%20to%20gain,Few%20calories%20or%20burn%20more.

Praderio, Caroline. "5 Reasons Your Smoothie Doesn't Taste Good (and How to Save It)." Prevention, 10 June 2019, www.prevention.com.

https://www.hsph.harvard.edu/nutritionsource/carbohydrates/fiber/#:~:text=Fiber%20is%20a%20type%20of,and%20blood%20sugar%20in%20check.

Farvid, et al. "Fiber." The Nutrition Source, 28 Oct. 2019, www.hsph.harvard.edu.

Franziska Spritzler, RD. "The Complete Guide to Sugar." Diet Doctor, Diet Doctor, 15 Dec. 2021, www.dietdoctor.com.

Stefani Sassos, MS. "There Are so Many Hidden Names for Added Sugar." Good Housekeeping, Good Housekeeping, 2 Nov. 2021, www.goodhousekeeping.com.

"Protein." The Nutrition Source, 12 Nov. 2021, www.hsph.harvard.edu.

By: and Shanna Mallon. "Types of Fruit: Fresh vs. Frozen." Vitamix.com, www.vitamix.com.

Myers, Dr. Amy, et al. "12 Benefits of Leafy Greens in Your Diet: Amy Myers MD ®." Amy Myers MD, NCBI, 17 Nov. 2021, www.amymyersmd.com.

"Understanding Antioxidants." Harvard Health, 10 Jan. 2019, www.health.harvard.edu.

Made in the USA
Coppell, TX
16 January 2025

44503242R00056